SHEA⌐
123 &

SPRING / SUMMER 2020

EDITOR
TONY FRAZER

Shearsman magazine is published in the United Kingdom by
Shearsman Books Ltd
P.O. Box 4239
Swindon   SN3 9FL

Registered office: 30-31 St James Place, Mangotsfield, Bristol BS16 9JB
(this address not for correspondence)

www. shearsman.com

ISBN 978-1-84861-719-3
ISSN 0260-8049

Subscriptions and single copies

Current subscriptions – covering two double-issues, each around 100 pages in length – cost £16 for delivery to U.K. addresses, £18 for the rest of Europe (including the Republic of Ireland), and £22 for the rest of the world. Longer subscriptions may be had for a pro-rata higher payment. Purchasers in North America will find that buying single copies from online retailers in the U.S.A. or Canada will be cheaper than subscribing. This is because airmail postage rates in the U.K. have risen rapidly, whereas copies of the magazine are printed in the U.S.A. to meet orders from online retailers there, and thus avoid the transatlantic mail.

Back issues from n° 63 onwards (uniform with this issue) cost £8.95 / $16 through retail outlets. Single copies can be ordered for £8.95 direct from the press, post-free within the U.K., through the Shearsman Books online store, or from bookshops. Issues of the previous pamphlet-style version of the magazine, from n° 1 to n° 62, may be had for £3 each, direct from the press, where copies are still available, but contact us for a quote for a full, or partial, run. With effect from the current issue, the single-copy retail price has risen to £9.95.

Submissions

Shearsman operates a submissions-window system, whereby submissions may only be made during the months of March and September, when selections are made for the October and April issues, respectively. Submissions may be sent by mail or email, but email attachments are only accepted in PDF form. We aim to respond within 3 months of the window's closure, i.e. all who submit *should* hear by the end of June or December, although for recent issues we have sometimes taken a little longer.

Acknowledgements

The poems by Celia Parra in this issue are drawn from her collection, *Pantallas* (Vigo: Galaxia, 2018).

This issue has been set in Bembo with titling in Argumentum. The flyleaf is set in Trend Sans.

Contents

Andrew Jordan

The Sea

Identifying with a force that no-one then could articulate,
I concealed myself amongst mysterious coercive things;
a slab of sombre fish, the cracked quartz of bloody ice
and slit belly of what lay cold. A rubbery, dissociated head.
Dazzled at the door, I paused and then, as always,
checked for reactions and cues that might imply rewards.

Now everyone agrees that beauty overlies an unknown power.
We all accede to love's ambivalence. And yet there was a time
when ideals, fully realised, did not imply regrets. Inscrutable sea,
I found my compromise in the love conditional, its dark and
fathomless complexities, commands and signs, and thus
immersed in it from early on, grew gills and fins and spines.

Amphitrite

The man caught by the tide, spewing water when they tipped his head,
intruded, passively, amongst the coloured balls and towels, the children
and the wives, of other people's holidays. But in being subject to a state
of erotic latency, as I was then, I stared at him, his vacancy, until
a lady, gentle and kind, insistent, introduced herself and turned me
from the water's edge. She said, "You don't really want to look at that…"

Pulling me along the beach, she showed me shells and stones within
still pools, whilst all the while I wanted to see that body. Her touch,
ambivalent, abides, yet years later I feel him there, still waiting.
With him, I'd wade into those overwhelming waves wanting
only to drown so she might find a life delivering the dead
or, transforming everything, cast me on the loins of that moist god.

Shanty

He was off the Gulf of Corryvreckan,
trapped beneath the sea. The seer saw
Myrddin Emrys rotating in a whirlpool,
split from himself, gone turning, turning
in a mass of cobalt seagreen bubbles.
As inhibitions hold the self constrained,
I had been for a long time lost, my self
bound by an unknown potentiality within
the awkward presence I could never own,
the absence that defined me
as other than I might have been.

I climbed on rocks, fumbled hooks through
lugworm, lobbed tackle where the heave died,
lured pollock and bream, pulled clots of wrack
and kelp through foam and then the rod
knocked in my hand and I saw it, head
clear, as I stretched forward; I gaped at
monstrous lips when, probing its guts,
turning the key, personified, it apprehended me.

Ever since, in moments of possession,
when picturing what I will shortly have,
I face the facts of my true nature and,
as I acknowledge them, re-enact, stunned,
what was still in my hand – fast within
it hides, and nothing escapes
those black, unblinking eyes –
I feel the weight of it.

   Coda
Were I, also, steadfast and vigilant, I'd never
have been caught by the bucking and writhing;
instead, in a flash, tilting the scales, I'd see
myself within that incomprehensible blur
and know my own ecstatic fall. Surfacing,

in my element, I would rejoice at the empty hand
and what had passed away, beyond its grasp.

Martin Anderson

Flowering Midnight

(For Mafruha)

> "She was walking like a Greek woman in Hades,
> like a Christian woman in Dante's *Inferno*, carrying
> a burden as old as History itself."
> —Marguerite Yourcenar

I

Under your collar
starched by the kiss of
flatirons I could smell
a faint scent, like amaretto
or oleander. Mixed
with that of Imperial Leather.

In an arbour, *hortus voluptatis*,
under the dusty boughs
of a linden tree, reclined on
a mossed bank, I imagined
I could hear, as you described
barricades thrown up in haste
at dawn across streets,
dogs bark. "The arbour is full
of noises" you said.

Who heard the bell
that struck the hour
of that midnight feast?
Under your roving hands
fragrant with flowers
there moved, through a grey
twilight, the face of one

I was fated to meet
one drear December
on the outskirts of a city dying
of boredom and fear.

Nails driven or pulled
what was the difference
in that midnight embrace
where solace was not
offered or asked for
and the heart wore
a tattered leaf shadow
a young girl's dress.

In the tedium
of unheated boudoirs
at midnight, cold
and disconsolate,
I counted the hours
waiting for you to arrive,
that sour spittle on your lip
a grape, your leg heavy
as a clod over mine.
A childhood of unassuaged
imaginings wrapped round
your little finger.

In darkness, I began
to suspect, only
did you truly open. Corolla
of empty slogan, cliché, catechism,
lullaby. A closed book:
to the inamorata in the ruined
garden, her vagabond
ghost sucking the dark
bitter pith of its fruit.
In a library of clear water,
a fountain, I saw your

inconsolable expression, heard
you mourning amidst the
apocrypha of each new dawn.

You came, slowly,
to resemble a blind man
stumbling amid ruins
of a past you did not understand.
As if you had dreamed it.
As if the pain of not being
there, in that *locus periucundus*, could
be quenched by tormenting another.
You expected me to dance
amid scattered spolia
to the faded choreography
of an illusion and to sing
to you like a fountain.
A dark ditch, rather,
to irrigate festering roses.

Days spent years later, after you
left on another fundraising and tour,
at the creek head. In a cloud
of mosquitoes, looking at water. Lights
flickered on and off at the shoreline.
Then stayed off: prison and army barracks
exhausting the grid with demands.
Night mingled the cry of victim
and sound of nightingale-thrush.
Over jagged inlet, wetland they floated.
Pain of convulsed limbs, torso
strapped down, merged with acme of
avian ardour. Some listened, offended
disturbed. Most did not.

You were midnight, I realised.
All along. In so many guises, places
and times. In seas of suffocating steerage

and oblivion. In plantations
of immense cruelty. Disavowed.
Your spoor, always changing
always the same. Towards the end
whenever you spoke in that high
pained voice you had perfected over
the years, of pique and irritable
opprobrium, I would hear the rattle
in drawing rooms of glass cabinets
opening. Full of antiques. Smell the stale
pomade of antimacassars eternally
whitening. You were like, I thought,
the old organ grinder on the corner
grinding out, year after year, the same
sad tune. Always, it seemed, at dusk.
On his threadbare clothes, as I passed,
I would smell the same sickly sweet
odour of roses that had never opened.

In a dusk of wood pigeons
and dust caked bowls of silent
fountains of an indebted estate,
on a bed of leaves beneath a tree
full of rotting oranges, they
(gardener and helpmate from
whom the rumour, soon scotched,
entered neighbouring towns)
had come upon you.
In flagrante delicto.
Thrusting, beneath the stained
tearings of a young girl's
dress, and groaning.
Your 'right': to demand
from an indigent's sirings
the youngest and earliest fruit
to spoil, in lieu of confiscation
of all he possessed. For which
no doubt later you would return:
your kind never getting enough.

II

Bright spurge and amaryllis.
A fragrant surrogate, an *arbor
Paradisi*, runs through all our days.
And like love, an old love, is, O
an old sore. Worked up,
under the collar, into
a poisonous malaise, it spreads.
Whored to prosperity, a bankrupt
pastoral: to the dictatorship of the rich.

III

I remembered days when he'd come back
smelling like a bunch of sweet grass:
dust of road, culm, attached
to him. Hand sweat tasting of
leather. Oil and unguent could erase
palm scars scored by reins. Redress
ravages of wind, sun. Too deep, though,
for them to erase, that shadow
midnight drew through my life. And draws
through the life of each of us and which,
like fallen angels, we can neither flee nor
acknowledge. Too deep for them, too,
to erase, that sound of dogs
tearing flesh in the scented arbour.
Delivered to them each day
until they'd developed a taste for it.
Staked out for them. Still talking:
while musicians played and ladies
under parasols, sipping cool
cordials, chattered and applauded.

He was my *daemon meridianus*
coming to lie with me,
"spell-stopp'd",

under the linden tree
in the cool breeze
bearing the scent of flowers
and incense. A dark breath-
ed censer dispensing endearments
into my heart. Bondage. Not bower.

And he was my north
ima praecipitari
turned into my south.
Wherever I turned to look
midnight masqueraded as dawn.
My true alignment became north.
So much so that night
deepened and whitened about me
removing 'impurities', 'stains'. All
opposites dissolved. A winnowing
of voices. Only his,
white cantor, dark tongue,
could be heard.

Under his collar,
halter, greasy white noose,
I inserted, at last, thumbs
and fingers and pulled. Tight. Till
those words liberté, egalité, fraternité,
sepulchres for bleeding ghosts,
choked in his throat. Saying:
"Broken philosophe, apothecary
no poultice, no potion, no salve
for the wound? Try this
garrot slowly turned, by one
of those with two legs
your kind first herded, penned."

Jennifer Spector

Hillside

Jaramillo Arriba, Chiriquí, Panamá

I

Volcán Barú bedding down
near indirect eruption
green & white depth marks
   impact sites   wind currents
                  clump extremes
a moving shed of residue

hybrid animal–human remains
   & admixed carpi
in states of crumbling alliance

II

not far from the village
Ngäbe girls in traditional dress
hold time in nacarat, heliotrope, emerald *naguas*
catch spires of straw heat
off the shelf   streaming the *bajareque*

      & water-borne guardians
rounding shifts travel as message
new wood   trace ceramic vessels   maps sketched
into stone   bone offerings by the foot
                  of the grave

sandbox tree that once held sand for ink
   also shaped *cayucos*, cattle fences
   & the huntsman's poisoned arrows
the miniature body smashing crude

14

objects
tapir or possum
honeybee hives in the river rush
&
cordillera

in a chain of connection

III

telluric energies
of last things

crops   old-growth forest
petroglyph sites   shamanistic reassembly
nest of the Quetzal

rifted
above ground
fragile schematics –

charted passage:
flutes from the femur   feathers
textiles   skin of jaguar & stones
to hold the body's timber

IV

aeolian   not far from the oak
lifts scat & tracks from the hide

place unearthed
& drifting
currach of body trawling
its load   shedding
natal distance

V

      & the rough house
     in mid-step moving
roots   grass & river
grafts what carried from
kyle & baleen to humic stratum

anchored by slim freight
sward still billeting green

Archer

first or second burial
soil stains unclear
as indicated by earth

a frottage of the body
disclaiming hull &
waterline by the hollows

ground-cloth and lacustrine
blades in a strike of shelter
small molds cupping The Three Graces

fletching the wind with summer's arrow
sienna pine scatters the floor
the *bajareque* peaks the mountain

mobility / tide / figure & landscape
interplay of relinquishing outlines

almost an outcry –
    January's unspent cloud
    trained on the mountain

Lisa Kelly

1,000 Words for Pictures on my
Samsung Galaxy S6 for 1,000 Torii Gates

As we move through torii, the gateway from the mundane to the sacred,
so experience moves through my camera phone to the recorded.

At Fushimi Inari-taisha, torii after torii – in the shrine there are thousands,
each gateway with a donor's black inked name – the cost in yen, thousands.

The vermillion Romon torii with three smiling women beneath.
Kenji caught off-guard, eyes shut, scowling, not showing his teeth.

Man, in sunglasses, jumper slung around his neck, holding his phone.
Woman with a white umbrella to shield her face from the sun.

The top half of a torii framed against the sky to cut out the crowd.
Flags and trees lining the concrete path under each bird abode.

Four of us in a line, mothers in the middle, flanked by sons.
An area demarcated by red and white bars balanced on white cones.

Three pigeons perched on the horizontal post of a torii.
In the far distance, the main shrine with its red and gold balcony.

Stone fox, kitsune, stares down with a stone granary key in its mouth.
Stone fox, kitsune, stares down with a stone rice ball in its mouth.

A kitsune, messenger of the gods, with a ceremonial bib around its neck.
A woman texting, she wears a shirt with bold black and white checks.

Curved temple roof to confuse evil spirits that travel in straight lines.
At the end of each beam, a gold square protector with a central flower design.

Seated figure of a samurai behind wire meshing and aquamarine posts.
Behind, fifteen arrows fan out, in the samurai's hands two arrows held crossed.

A bald man rings a bell to bring luck, two women with rucksacks wait.
One wears a flat cap, the other a hijab, both ready with coins to donate.

The main hall, honden, with two Shinto priests, one standing, one kneeling.
Girl in olive green trousers and short-sleeved white shirt, bowing.

Wooden wishing plaques, ema, with orange sun and leaping wild boar.
Messages in Kanji and English displayed in haiden, the offerings hall.

Close up of Caitlin's card wishing for happiness, health and prosperity.
Pamela from the US asks for 'Love & Peace' for friends and family.

Amber wishes for a full life full of love, good health and happiness.
I can read Masayo's name, not her wishes, but guess they include happiness.

Plaques hang off hooks in orange slats of wood by doubled purple cord.
In the picture, twenty are fully visible, eight are semi-obscured.

Start of the Senbon Torii trail, a torii with peeling paint and a scuffed base.
Kenji's black medical mask and white tracksuit hood hide his face.

The back of a girl's head – I will never know more – with long, brown hair.
Selfie with my son in his Nike hat trying to look like he's not there.

Dane swigging from a bottle of peach flavoured water, his earphones in.
Leaf litter on the grey pebbles, exposed roots of trees to the side of him.

More backs as we follow the path and a baby in a sling in a yellow hat.
Woman in kimono with red flowers, a white flower holding hair in a plait.

Woman in kimono with red flowers smiling at her friend dressed the same.
One holds a pale basket, her friend holds one the colour of yellow grain.

The bamboo trunks in row after row, spears breaking into an eggshell sky.
A picture of the bamboo grove angled from below to show just how high.

Kenji in profile, looking up at treetops, his right hand on a slim bamboo bole.
Stem rings mark each segment, carved messages mark a need to assert the soul.

Small shrine with a bell and steps up to a statue of a kitsune with its red bib.
Is this where kami spirits of rice, tea, Sake, fertility, agriculture and success live?

Dappled sunlight turning patches on posts from vermillion to gold.
A torii stripped back to the original wood with swathes of green mould.

Woman with a dark blue and maroon sash wrapped around her kimono.
Tiny white flowers on the bag carried in the crook of her elbow.

A shrine on the trail, a little entrance, and no-one there. Or is it a café?
Thirteen steps to a large torii. Go through to shop selling small wooden torii.

Solitary man with a backpack, he is looking at torii and foxes. What to buy?
A water fountain, temizu, with a bamboo chute and scoop to purify.

Proof of the summit: you are here in English and Kanji on the wooden map.
The picture of the four of us – perfected using BeautyPlus filter app.

A second picture of the map with text you are flipped to mirror image text.
Symbol of the man at the summit now has his left arm raised north–west.

Kyoko and I in front of two women in flowery kimonos. We are in black.
Leaning on a balcony overlooking mountains, our hair blowing back.

A gold triceratops charm dangles from my neck, a silver bangle hangs loose.
Kyoko has a fine gold chain around her neck, in her ears are gold hoops.

Rabbits ears behind Kyoko's head; Dane making the Victory sign.
A hazy sky, modern grey buildings of Kyoto, mountains, the treeline.

Son's Selfie with 'SUNDAY FUNDAY' filter in purple, yellow and red.
Torii over steps down Mount Inari, Dane looks back, eyes shadowed.

Descending steps with four backs in the picture, one man against the flow.
His left knee juts forward, the sole of his shoe forever facing the view below.

'Champion' written across Kenji's white hoodie in dark blue text.
The setting sun overscored by parallel power lines, a final torii frames our exit.

At Fushimi Inari-taisha, torii after torii – in the shrine there are thousands,
each gateway with a donor's black inked name – the cost in yen, thousands.

As we move through torii, the gateway from the mundane to the sacred,
so experience moves through my camera phone to the recorded.

Nathan Shepherdson

mixed memory on paper
Whiteley visits Morandi

when he died
i found me
living in my room
until now

until your head
falls into your lap
you will not see yourself
first hand

the second reality
in a third string field
attached to nothing
describes no one
to himself

a white heron
prepares to sip gravity
from a ceramic bottle
in Bologna

in complete privacy
a sample
however small

nothing is more alien
than art in the work of art
in itself

by avoiding the metaphysical
i grow fingernails
in the light

his glass womb
the perfect vessel
for silent opera

a life might only be
as long as the arm
you paint with
write with
or inject

there is no passage
to where you are
if you're there
telling yourself not
to breathe until
the disease captured
by sun in the window
is cured so theory
can forget why
it exists and comfortably
finish its speech
in the empty room
where saints continue
to polish the floorboards
by blinking

there are lessons
that burn the candle
the other way

this illusion at peace
with what it resents
allows skin to sleep
unattached to any form

three sisters in the shape
of a wife i will never have
thankfully take turns to rinse

my eyelids to leave them hang
on the back of a chair

all density sent to all corners
as i insert the fingertip
into subconscious surface

removing it
the energy returns
so i can remove myself

too relaxed
at the prospect of death
i realise i have never
found a head that suits
my appearance

on a palette the shape of a brain
dust legislates in tones
as organised as undecided time
kept deep in the glandular biology
of a simple brush

involuble pigments
set under the resonance
of a linseed cello

words cannot be trusted
in the company of art

tell a painting what it is
it will know you are lying

my method is to fill
canvas bags with memory
place them at the foot of the door
then calmly wait for the flood
i am told will never arrive

my purpose to defend colour from its ego

on an unsigned postcard of my work
sent to me by myself i read...

he had stopped working;
was going blind;
was readying himself for death;
had never visited Paris;

in sympathy i stretch out full length
on the table to observe the last pear

my nose an intimate companion
pressed to the hip of its ripening ballast

its solitary leaf
curled to its stem
in dry surrender

when they cut the tree down
the sap ran from the limbs
of my childhood

clouds that are still alive are still dead in here

to paint what i can see is to see what i cannot paint

a mirror is the ransom note anyone can read
but nobody chooses to pay

we kidnap ourselves by being alive

Notes
—The stanzas commencing 'in complete privacy' and 'nothing is more alien'
use manipulated fragments from a 1958 interview with Giorgio Morandi
by Edouard Roditi.
—The stanza 'he had stopped working' uses a quote from a notated drawing
of Morandi by Brett Whiteley. Whiteley visited Morandi in 1960, noting
that Morandi was upset because his favourite pear tree had been cut down.

Simon Perchik

★

In the slot for tracks the time between trains
is your last address though it's the station
that's waiting for the years gone by to return

the way this unwanted newspaper is already seated
as if it was going further and at the border
would spread as the grammar all travelers learn

from each other to put the minutes in order
before reaching out to hand some conductor
the death certificate that has no period

for the hole to be dug by the silence
reaching out from so many tears
night after night for it to end.

★

You work this bottle cap the way the early Earth
turned then emptied for the first tide
that now follows it one death at a time as the silence

that cannot be cured — it's a small pill and twice a day
smells from the shallows reaching out from a sea
that no longer moves though you tilt your head

side to side as if its primordial sequence
was still in place, waiting to drain the glass
while you are leaning over the sink from so far away

and because you have two lips you bite down to spit
as if the splash would loosen the label used to scab
that never heals when you swallow each pill for later.

★

You opened this umbrella slowly, sure
what it wants is already circling
as the mountainside you carry around

for an overhang – under this hidden grave
it's easy to stay dry when there's some stone
unfolding your arms the way each death

comes here as rain to put out the rain
burning alive in your arms
that have so much to do with opening

and closing though what was once a branch
still tries to shake its dead leaves back to life
by reaching out as shade and trembling.

★

Side by side, your weakest finger
is taken from you, becomes the echo
flowing out one hand

as the darkness with a straight line
– you point to shine light on the shadow
that's slowly moving toward you

the way every death is remembered
for its emptiness reaching in
where it once was, wanting

to be held between both hands, twisted
as the cry for lift before shattering
into stars you can no longer hear.

★

You learn by kneeling in the rain
for a heart to form – this puddle
is already gathering another

as if the sun was still giving birth
though August is nearly over
has slowed its turn the way rings in a tree

keep track how long it takes to gather tears
from its silence and in your eyes
bring them together as moonlight

– you can hear the word
long before it leaves your mouth
is sobbing on the ground

that was once your lips, spread out
for the trembling that forgot
how to say goodbye, lean over and sweat.

Amlanjyoti Goswami

The future arrives at a Boston hotel

By the hotel, the car park,
By the car park, the wind, the backyard
Of a departmental store

Beside which is hunger and midnight
And no food and sound of clapping thunder.
The wind goes on, it bites, the rain lashes

Deep inward thoughts. They strike at the throat.
Makes you remember tropical sunrises
Hot days of May when stepping out spelled danger.

You want to go on walking, go on to the sea shore
Where lives eternity, etched in blue and white,
Where you can't tell the difference.

But the wind won't let you. The wind and that fear you carry
That makes you build houses, look for food,
That doesn't like the smell of danger

Your shadow nearby. Your own ghost prowling the night.
You are forced back in, inside the hotel
Into routine, central heating, good evening

Into the lift carrying yourself, doors opening,
A lonely room with writing pad, lit desk, carpet,
Thoughts of home, wherever it is.

Frequent tossing turning, abandonment that accompanies
Being left alone.
Staring the blinds down – outside, used car repairs in need of repair

An odd car passing by, afraid for its own future,
The future, what it became, and how
It arrived so early.

Shoe Hospital

Roadside corner
Once you crossed Spectacle Repairs.

Outside, just a rack
Where they lay cooped up

Tongue deep in trouble.
Wear and tear of everyday

Drag and grind of road,
Dust and stone, chipping at the years

Reclining arterial walls, soft skin pore,
Spirit soles, or sole spirit

A tear melancholic, epidermal,
Deeper woes inside.

Only when you peered inside
The grim sorrow of a common ward,

No place to sit, all beds taken.
The antiseptic anticipation

Something good about to happen,
Fear it isn't going well.

Skin to skin, mouth to mouth
Kiss of life, spit and shine.

Sewn with string, held surgeon tight.
The knife through the bone

Of affliction unknown.
Nothing shows up, though all the signs are there.

Inside out, straggling,
Or in neat rows, rested.

The good cobbler on his midnight rounds
With mallet, hammer and thread

Humming a low tune, muttering something
About wellness   breathing deep   making haste slowly.

Chris Holdaway

Gorse

Star tetrahedron – gorse is evergreen – everyone of us
Growing into spines and thorny families. Something is
Concealed – hedges of our colonial nursery – standalone
Windbreaks now the good missionaries have gone by
Turning into everyone else not leaving. The universal culture
Of rent rose from the ocean. Sovereign pacifists in alien land
Of land alienation confronting the thirdhand or worse
Reports of someone else's vision. As yet the creature of office
Come face to the mysteries of intensified agriculture –
Witness in wheat stalks reinforcing concrete to the first tree
Cut down. A century's new growth from boiler felled trunk
Thine everpresent bloom in the vacuum of cleared ground
Thine evergreen nevertheless a personification of land
In drought – temperate cactus – the green scaffolding of
Another world. All oppressions are essentially questions
Of geometry from phrenological survey to voting electorates.
All calendars worth of nature propaganda would have you
Bury the mine tailings under acid green pasture yourself
– a smile of powerlines under a rainbow switching between
Markers of civilisation and charges of uncontested loneliness.
Ulex of the northern south and eastern west – points of light
By which to chart rank settlers who placed thy fearful heavens
On the ground in lieu of stone walls. Stunted pine you lash out
Never to be fit for forestry and how many workers lost
Fingers to manufacture the world's supply of gorse? Rip tooth
Of the bank's deforestation – given yet its catacomb roots
To incubate native brush until a forest bursts from the chest.
Immutable presence as assured as debt...
    I'm trying to spend more time with my breath held in
Than holding the world at bay – to turn the height of
Drawing in to my relaxed point of rest – swallowing gorse
In a sword act filling my bloodstream like a cast mould.
With all these cuts on my hands how it smarts just to hold

A piece of fruit – the very picture of closeness amidst spines
Yet the pain of decision ever branching in thy drive –
And I feel badly for the space everything is always pushing
Out of the way. The scene of countless germinations without
Bothering with the tragedy of change.

Heritage pamphlet

In the heart of construction you'd like to think
There is some pride of place besides a crown
Poorly translated. The only way to survive
Is to believe the land was nothing
But idle before the townhalls built like theatres
– the old theatres gutted to set up shop –
Never to think who says the sweat off my back
And the soot in my lungs are at once
The mortar between your bricks and the decay
That exhausts them. Historic mosaic floor
Forgotten and rediscovered only when even
The dust that buried it became a necessary
Building material. Of all things sand
Used for land reclamation is running short
Spurring underground markets and this flash
Part of town named for a bay no longer rests
On worker's cottages pushed into sea like
Embalming sawdust and setting sun.
A wharf still exists under the road – buried
Prince – the sugarcoated hills replaced by large
Cruise ships. The waterfront boardwalk is
Inlaid with ornamental fossils and shells and
After an immeasurable length archaeologists
Find our remains among them. The discovery
Becomes a touchstone for all contemporary art
– sombrely poignant yet charmingly meta –
That this ancient race understood the long
Game of fossilisation well enough to include
Representations in their own graves. My bodily

Waste by now mostly enamel housepaint but I
Don't understand any of these buildings well
Enough to jump off them – to be caught up in
Lime trees lining stately streets as a telltale mark
Of decline in one of the original theories of
History. We didn't have the authority required
To truly bridge water other than with true bridges
To nowhere. As if faded grandeur were built in
From the start of knotted weatherboards as key
-stones in all our attempts at grandiose arches.
Who saw through the military bases for what
They were – bastions protecting only their own
Gates. Cut your own grass from the waists of state
Engineers. To walk as protest over the paved-over
Trail of tears.

G.C. Waldrep

[Additional Eastnor Poem (vii)]

Thunder must have a hygiene
I emptied the last milk from the bottle, into my mouth
Rinsed the bottle, came that much closer
To immanence
That much closer to the lilac bough
The reliquary, dented & tarnished, was disappointing
We'd had to ask to see it
We'd had to request an audience with the sea
Detached head of the mauled capercaillie by the track
Vermilion head of the dispatched capercaillie
A communion that takes place in the eye
But is not of the eye
To which the eye is merely witness
A signatory, as to some will or deed, a transfer
Two hikers passed me on the path, then two cyclists
Their garments almost exactly the same
Earlier I'd plunged my hand into the heated basin
The wild aurora above my dream-village
Flickering off & on, on & off
I have never, to my knowledge, dreamed of flies
I rinsed the bottle, placed it on the lit sill to dry
Matter murmurs into matter
Like the music of harps, a constant inturning, a key
Possession is nine-tenths of history, my friend
Admonished, from Alaska
Having been, as I note here, a student of possession
I lifted the smell of my own body in both hands
As if it were heavy
As if the ritual, like a garden, required tending
The bonfires, appearing in the distance, frightened me
They burned mauve in the dusk
I shaved my upper lip again, as per custom
Acquired from our time in one of many wasted plains

We are reluctant to relinquish it
We pay the same prices in the stores that you do
What remains unaddressed (in this poem)
Is music, the problem of music
Which is not the same as the problem of fatherhood
Some men manage both, simultaneously
I admire those men
One visited the disused chapel yesterday
While I, unbeknownst to him or to his wife, paused
Behind a screen
He sung a few lines of an ancient hymn, for his wife
That's one I learned on the island, he told her
Soon they strolled away (as did I, tactfully, a bit later)
Of all the things I could have left there
I wanted a shell, from the sea, but I had no shell
It has been many years now since I walked by the sea
I would not describe myself as unhappy
Only devastated
The unbroken vastness of the ear
Represented perfectly by that painter on canvas
Twilight tones, he called them
He had trekked that spring from town to northern town
Keeping a diary as a pledge against sleep
His canvases were another matter, those he sold
In the little markets as in the great houses
Where his friends introduced him (to their friends)
Now we have his versions
Of a horse's head, a lilac bough
Of milk, of a dune, of a copse in the midst of a storm
Wild with lightning (& with his emblem of lightning)
Rendered in his hand
With which it is said he once saved a child
From drowning, or was it a fire, no one is quite sure

[Additional Eastnor Poem (ix)]

Let's break the camera's coal, you said to me
I leaned back against planes
Of brute experience
I'd inherited, as from some father's father
We were friends, you see, the winds knew us
I almost knew your other name
Though within our maculate soliloquies
We often approached the sacred
As through a succession of enamelled plates
Chladni had the right idea
Induce a vibration, watch where dust settles
Watch where the gold burns itself into the sea
Of thinking, of names
We were guests at the execution, we bore
Our invitations in the notches of each right ear
Such splendid pageantry
When the corpse leapt up, duly dampened
Let's break that corpse, you said to me
But I pretended I hadn't heard
I pretended I had known capitalism's precincts
I pulled my garment more tightly around
My head
This was all not so long ago
We had both studied, we had both assisted
The prisoners
With their broths & gruels
What then can be said of the heart, the muscle
Whose fist, like a low-slung island
Punches again & again at the gilded thorn
Let's consult the witnesses, you said, & then
I nodded, I consented
I agreed:
Truly, let us go, let us consult the witnesses
Not realizing you were speaking of ourselves
The ruins we had fostered
The silks we had touched, & stained

Being held for us now in all the best museums
Profane veronicas
I can't even begin to describe
What the water felt like, when my body hit
In full view of the cameras of earth, fire, & air

[Additional Eastnor Poem (x)]

*

Long light of the northern sky, stand by my bed
I have no other use for you
I shake my phylacteries in your thousand faces
You lave my limbs with your thousand tongues

Ralph Hawkins

Roman Holiday

walk the Trastevere
green shoots in clamour
stripped swimming
sticky-buds on the tide
linger to watch
as birds fly off
marble stele
a fountain of turtles
and you are elsewhere
thinking new false
nails stiletto nude
hawks & sparrows
in a cloud they
rise winging it
outside the Basilica
of Our Lady
for a few euros
walking later to
Gramsci's grave
in the fine rain
please take heart
and hold my hand

in celluloid
you return to me
thin as a stick bloated
clouds glum &
downcast condole
in flights of fancy
I am weak
pasty as pastry
& cry too soon

taking the wafer of
love into my mouth
sceptre, mantle, dewy
gem, chewy mints &
fancy cakes
O where did you go
I loved you
muffling my face
like a trapped door
portico & night safe

wash after sex
and use a condom
avoid harsh soaps
& douching little
calves spindle thin
with stiff knees
how shall I dream
of you now
in what linted field
& my soul yours
how shall it rest
when the bedsheets
have been bundled
& the day rumpled
by the lumpen
shrieking & hammering
to free the caged birds
linnet, siskin, wren
the leaves billow
at night with more
unfinished business
poppy milk & shower
making a clean
breast of it

James Bell

Some stations of Hiroshige's Tōkaidō Road

Nihonbashi Bridge – 1st station

after dawn no hustle and bustle
   words not heard
      a rose tinted wisp of mist

below Mount Fuji
   herds its bulk upwards once more
      unnoticed on Nihonbashi Bridge

some begin their day with heavy bundles
   cross in an opposite direction
      to the nobleman's progress

all feet sound on the wooden bridge
   in soft or loud percussion
      you cannot hear them

in the vanguard of a nobleman
   only one face looks your way
      in this train of sons brothers fathers

below there are no ripples on Sumida River
   the barge and its master are in stasis –
      Hiroshige (hard g) has learnt perspective

houses on either bank become smaller
   incrementally while moored boats
      do likewise in a cumulative V-shape

behind the centre of the bridge –
   two men lead with white plumes on poles
      that imitate black trees in the distance

all walk towards impossible futures in Kyoto
    two women who carry panniers walk into
        the present from the opposite direction

Shinagawa – 2nd station

a classic three part image

first the main street of the village
    wooden houses - open fronts show tatami
        all parts of an inn

citizens – vendors – travellers walk this street
    turquoise like the sea beyond
        it all runs at an angled tilt

between Kyoto and Edo – no words
    sea in the next part flat
        only your eyes reach for a third dimension

size is important - for large boats at anchor
    two at sail reach for another world
        three skiffs squat in steps – head for shore

a spit with another village stabs the sea
    dark and light – the straight horizon
        rose and red sky announces dusk

another day in Shinagawa

Kawasaki - 3rd station

many years before internal combustion
   there are boats to transport ordinary people
      who would fear much more than sails in the wind
         and poles for skiffs pushed into the bottom
            of this bay

where more boats surround the edges –
   a scene interested in movement on calm water
      on people passing on the shoreline path
         in the foreground

a stall nestled on the left among dark green trees
   has one customer whose neck bends forward
      to stare at the wares before him –
         there's light enough to see inside

trees thrust into a sky becoming dusk
   slivers of mist in the distance announce nightfall
      boats arrive and no others leave
         porters still walk with bundles

horizontal lines pervade the central bay
   illustrate backs and forths while
      distant lines prepare to come forward
         as steps towards the future

soon travellers and villagers will rest
   not knowing that the world turns all night

Jennifer K. Dick

Masthead

1

to choke and cross back
from underworlds / whorls
the deep-diver's record
122 meters in 4 mns 22secs
dépassant / dépaysement
in different time zones
meridians mucus microcosms
platforms unequivocally
distributed like catch phrases
longitudinal exoskeletons
equitable consequence's escape
balance (verse—vibrations—vibrato)
and of marble
soapstone — sand salt
crystals lost on her
tongue alongside the
diminishing value
of…

2

lost field reports sightings
olive-green underwater
imprints: waves, skies
accounts of sundry afternoons
with his mistress her
lover the pool boy the
charge of prostitution
what sticks to the soul
is emblazoned upon lapels
the sins of

and farther, adrift,
the forgotten
foretold / telling

3

torqued transience
above, on the trapeze,
(she) is flight a
bright binge-released
lover confetti-stars scattering
into the choking crowd
beholden to
hours

4

acquiesce to accounts
frozen finances gridded
predictions line each section
of passing economies
"brut et net" in French
taxed de-escalation
via negotiations
third party tribute
or tribes: reports
pasted rectangular
like surround-sound
Dolby in the center afloat
respite if only
she could climb aboard
row or rows
awaiting / away

5

form formulae Formica-
lined rooms she batters

her head like a ram
against the leisure
vs. culture sections:
in today's news
erasures, water laps
at language stealing off
letters: verbs and nouns,
the accounted-for linguists
lurking among
the drowned

6

fundamental motions of
clarity, proximity, toxicity
to stave off or starve
the room of visions /
visitors: the exhibition
temporarily closed
for problematic abuse of
dimensional and time-
travel portals:
measure the returns, the
stacks of evidence,
the force of each body
comatose
which refuses its own
release

7

mutter countdowns
clavicle enclave columbine
and daisies dished out
drivel or vases: draconian
decor placating pleas
ideas / ideals
sounded out in

the want-ads:
promises of love predicated
on horoscopes
or back-page funnies
grip the gold key
tugboat-rise rowboat flight
cresting, affixed
in space
land
ho!

Hazel Smith

Screenshots

A daft French divorcee is scavenging for new lovers. A father and son road-movie dissolves in armchair yawning. A bespectacled American fashion icon loudly stylish in her nineties. Resolving an insult in Lebanon when there is reluctance to concede. A lesbian relationship as nuclear bomb in an orthodox Jewish community. A fragile German transsexual sways between gossamer identities. A young victim of an acid attack celebrates her immutable burns. A love affair consorts tragically with the heat of the cold war. An exposé of Australian racism through the boos that bully applause. An Israeli soldier travels to Paris to shake off his allegiances. A woman secretly ghost writes her husband's feted novels. A young girl falls in love with a self-deluded drug addict. Aretha Franklin in concert. Nureyev's defection to the west. An old school Pakistani father, a son who craves to write. A Palestinian poet activist suddenly disappears. Thought to be an Islamic terrorist but, in reality, brutally murdered. Violent, compromised photos. Bruises on her lover's arms. The scenes play out to a bathetic but operatic soundtrack. Tariq becomes Ricky, then Ricky turns more radical. In the background, if you can find him, a young and sensual Mick Jagger.

Off Limits

he said let's not mix up sexism and out of line behaviour
she showed an eccentric devotion to appliances and cleaning
once you have a theory you just wait for it to be confirmed
if he had solved the DNA enigma they would not have cheered
      the result
wealth is a quiet stock, he said, while income is a noisy flow
peaches are delicious but the cost differs from impeachment
they measured out her isolation cell within the closeted courtroom
don't leave me she reiterated though the words drew loneliness closer
she perfected the art of making everything sound alluring and decisive
they traded a fake silence for an acoustics that enhanced the violence

I would never have done anything to hurt her, the suspect inexplicably said
the pain she endured arose from the bedside manner perpetuated by others
a man is suing his parents because his birth has brought him suffering
she was bored with the debates about whether computers could sob
        and sigh and rage
the feedback cello soaks up a range of self-resonating behaviours
though not ill she was asked repeatedly to expound on her diagnosis

Artistic License

he always had a dozen or more paintings
in a state of nervous germination
hanging in his studio

the walls a dense swirl
of highly-coloured possibilities
emergent lives strapped to different stages

he would stride from one to the other
salting and shaking them
a dab here, a wipe there

or just stand, absorb and cogitate
before moving on to the latest victim
next beneficiary

while he was working on one
he could spy
the other oils obliquely

sense their distracted
low-pitched presence

unconscious exercise
in wall to wall communing

mainly abstractions
they embraced
smears and whisperings
wheels and clocks
religious icons

sometimes the paintings
would hang for months or years
in the underworld between start and finish

sometimes a painting
seemed to refuse delivery

as if it were gestating
an undernourished myth
a half-formed opinion

then suddenly his hand would
know how to pull it to fruition

though what did "finished" mean?

paintings that seemed mature to others
remained howling infants to him

he needed to rescue them
before they prematurely aged
or belatedly aborted

often, they morphed effortlessly
into other voluble beings

the most unobliging rehabilitated as
the most hospitable

Peter Robinson

Cross Country

'Nulla dies sine linea'
  —Pliny the Elder

Never a day without a line;
but on this later train
taking in the marginal and left behind
constituencies, again I think
of standing still an hour for some signalling mistake,
like we had taken a wrong train or line,
and, timetables out of sync,
been advised to alight at Leamington Spa –
the station at which we waited
on that interminable journey back home
to find I'm forever identified, there,
with how it was we'd stepped to the platform
breathless and exasperated.

On schedule through Leamington, Banbury, each station
of the CrossCountry service today,
a polite old lady with a Geordie accent
inquires 'How far are you travelling today?'
and I'm moved by the musical chairs
when someone appears with a seat reservation;
then slowing beside what remains
from Didcot's half-demolished power station,
our train, suffused by the sunset glow
crawls on its fixed timetable,
and still nobody's able
in the lingering twilight's extended shadow
to tell how far we're to stay or go.

29 March 2019

Though Spring Is Here

'as naturally as the leaves to a tree'
   John Keats

'History touched me *en passant*.'
   Alexander Shurbanov

Cloud-forms are blushing at an early dusk
and a chill wind's driven in from the north
casting clouts about this May
on washing lines, wind ruffling
that sycamore's leafage a-flicker
with late sun and your feeling
all over the shop, like that laundry, those leaves,
has you glance at two women discussing the foxgloves
or a border's viable, timely plantings
beyond lit reading lamp and things
cluttering its table surface –

old age's forgetfulness in place
amongst the close-packed furniture…
Now as mental spaces open
you're really not that sure
it's about that tree, true, or that truth is
caught in the leaves' bright narrow gaps;

but still its wind-stirred, sunlit tops
might lift the stressed, the ill-at-ease,
leaving them in peace, with trees,
as you watch leaf-shadow on a garden wall
sustain and stay, or not at all.

Rosanna Licari

Ascendancy

For Else Marie Friis, botanist and paleontologist

It began at the peripheries.
The flower took advantage
edging into the domain
of the conifer and fern.
Sporting tiny, crumpled faces,
bulb-like and unremarkable,
their early Cretaceous selves
gave no clue as to
the vibrant chroma
of future progeny.

Angiosperm
– *seed in vessel*
the core
a compact mechanism,
designed for proliferation.
Pollen encased in the inner chamber
triggers the venture.
The seed forms and anticipates
the unfurling dance
of germination.

Darwin puzzled over
the 'abominable mystery'
but it was the petal
that gave the push forward
when diversity
brought the overlooked to the attention
of those that mattered.

Reshaped, variegated and audacious,
they lured insects

which crawled over
the plant and its flowers.
A mutually beneficial arrangement.
The great radiation spurred on
by coevolution.
Pollen everywhere.

The fruit eaten, was digested.
Seeds dropped
behind the lumbering dinosaurs
that ploughed up the earth.

A communal garden.
Sovereignty clinched
without a fight.

Note: Flowering plants were the extreme exception to Darwin's notion that evolution occurs gradually, that natura non facit saltum, *nature does not make a leap.*

Disappearing Act

Discarded after a show
her husband brought
all ten doves home
to save them.
He's not a magician.

White and beautiful
but too old now
for another performance.
Too much cooing.
Courtship disturbs.
Size matters.
A distraction from the tricks.

She put them in the coop
with the hens.
Two died and
a friend made a pet
of the male:
a blessing.
Can't set them free.
Can't fly properly.
No homing instinct.
Not made for the outdoors.
The lucky seven live
for the moment.

Meghan Purvis

Dan Fucking Duryea

Would not like the title of this poem,
Dan was kind from everything I hear.
There's a story about his son at a premiere
hearing someone call his character a sonofabitch
and the kiddie standing on his seat and yelling
you take that back, that's not my daddy

It's too pat to point out it's always somebody's
daddy; Dan chewed his way through a lot but
I feel confident he'd be still and nod his head
to that one. Because Dan Duryea was a stand-up
guy, we all know this, all of us who pay attention
to actors like Dan Duryea, but we also know

how things turn, how the man you counted on,
the man you love can turn around and swing. Maybe
with an open palm, like how Dan did it, that last
pull back, but maybe not, and that's where the music rests,
where you never quite know. A man can love you,
love your legs down to the ground, but when things

get tight he'll leave you without thinking twice about it,
leave you to the back of a squad car, to Eddie Robinson
fishmouthing at you over breakfast for the next twenty years,
to a knife slicing through a sheet straight at you
and it's what you deserved all along, he just hadn't quite
got around to telling you. But you knew all the time,
didn't you, deep down girls like you always know.

At the Organ

The road and everything begins to smell cut-lemon bright
and dipped in salt, scrubbing. A kitchen on a spring morning
with window-glass so clean it shines like a blade.
This is the topnote, the kiss with lips just parted

for the moist breath in between to get you interested,
to make you lean in. Inhale deep. Next the base:
the smell of bodies, of new sweat, sweetness
with a thrum of sour milk beneath, a baby's room.

When you turn the corner and the scent of blood opens
is the full chord, emerging in a metallic shock
against the city clean-up van, exhaust and meat
twined around soapy water a glum man in a coverall
hoses off the road. The morning verges on too beautiful.

This is how to make perfume: make something smell human
and smash it. Scrub your house until your knuckles shred
and the walls shine, this is how we start, until your bucket
gleams dark enough to scry in. Topnote, basenote, heart.

Abegail Morley

For remembrance

I love my chosen names; zip and unzip them from my neck
as if I can reveal two bodies simultaneously, let down
a sheath of blonde hair only I can clamber up. I think

of you, mother, registering my birth. The awkward pen
slipping your grip, the silence of the page fumbling
beneath black ink, that radio song in the back of your mind,

heady as Jasmine. I think of you moisturising your belly
and your soap-scrubbed body and the woman who
imagined her world would not be this. I think of you

with your sawn-off tongue so you wouldn't tell,
breasts stoked with milk, and I know how hard it is for you
to let me go, when I've kicked and kicked to see daylight.

Bed

Moths unslick themselves from pupa and in my skull
their wings a delicate dust like a mid-summer burial plot
when digging stops and worms have shunted and shunted
to the very end of the earth. The vicar secretly pleased
of his windblown "dust to dust". I feel a light flutter
on furred temporal lobes as wings fall mute like a leaf
stalling mid-air. In these soft-morning hours
I rehearse the day, my lampshade face unlit, words
stuck tight in the porthole of my mouth. Once I woke
as the sun, a fibre-optic tree, a Catherine Wheel,
body blinking with constellations. I was everything rapid
in the heart of this bed that burnt torso-ash and pillows
sunk to a black hole, and depression clanged its bell.

Sarah Barnsley

I agree to read all the terms and conditions

to the point of exhaustion: please, give me a thesis-length
volume of them, daily, add this to my list of duties and
do not compensate me for the extra hours, request that
all terms and conditions are printed in 8 point font and
recommend that I purchase a customised magnifying glass
from a preferential online company which will involve
further terms and conditions to agree to in order to conduct
a fair examination of the thesis-length vols. now accelerating
their rate of arrival to three times a day, now in 6 point font.

I agree to carry out the necessary actions required in order to
complete the tick boxes at the end with professional integrity.
These include: (i) successful completion of one undergraduate
law degree; (ii) a postgraduate diploma in business and finance;
(iii) psychiatric screening to assess capacity to make complex
decisions in a given timeframe; (iv) certification as an instructor
in a sport or leisure pursuit for added breadth; (v) acceptance for
additional borrowing to cover the costs of (i) to (iv) above; and
(vi) new ability to lie about what I am doing with my time.

In agreeing to all terms and conditions, I understand that it is
my responsibility to ensure that: (a) all possible nuances of
meaning are detected/held in my head for as long as I shall
live; (b) there is no violation of obscure pieces of international
legislation past/present; (c) next door's chickens are put
away each night/their recycling bin out on alternate Fridays;
(d) the pavements are free from broken glass and all our children
can walk safely down them/their parents need never worry again;
(e) all those who have ever been poisoned are now un-poisoned;
(f) all those who have swallowed batteries now unswallow them;
(g) people who cannot remember when they last took their pills
now remember them, with no possibility of accidental overdose;
(h) every effort is made not to cry in supermarket cafés/
commuter trains/the office/in front of partner and child

The other side of the

She said it once crossed her mind
checked it out, dismissed it

I look in the mirror
the facial hair
the moustache

this central defender's build
the body I buy men's clothes for
no *hormonal imbalance, take metformin*

My mind is blown
the reluctance to look at people
being in groups, a team at work even

I used to think
companionable but not good-looking
kicked like a football by my previous owners

Yet we both know
I haven't responded well to training
can only sit long enough for treats
a furry cloud fallen to the ground

I could be a bison, I've grazed their plains

It explains everything
how in biology I'm a ruminant

quarter panel mirror

that I was a buffalo,
but what if she was right?

the signs are there:
a velvety snout,
a tuft damp with nostril juice;

all shoulders, no hips, thin legs,
the shape of a map of America,
just features natural to buffalos.

it now makes sense:
the endless walking for I don't know what,
saying nothing, neck lowered to grass.

I was probably a dog:
a cleaned-up, rescued mongrel,
lovable, now, to a kind woman.

there's no canine in me:
in all our time together,
before I balloon into brown,
too heavy to stay up.

but more accurately I'm a buffalo.

the public comedy of my looks,
how in fear I might stampede.

Matthew Stoppard

Killing a rat with an air rifle

toothy librarian in the crosshairs
belly of pure white fur   not as dirty as they say you are
neighbours watching me
stooped low on the lawn   children in the window
the squeal and wriggle when the pellet hits
more forgettable than your lifeless tail   hard and leathery
every wire and shoelace unbearable   kettles and laptops
                                              connected to you
in the walls
pinching it to take you from patio to wheely bin   a pallbearer
felt every time I tie my boots

I remember air cadets   learning to shoot a man
with 100 for a heart   missing each time
so why can I hit you   the size of my son's cuddly toy
moving at the speed of thought

Riding the stang*

Here we come with ran, dan, dang;
It's not for you, nor for me, we ride this stang
But for Gooseberry Bob, whose wife he did bang.

ladles pound saucepans
like Mum being thrown against the wall
between your bedroom and hers

to keep the rabble at bay
you tear out rain-wrinkled images
first found behind Kwik Save

arthritic pang of a reader's wife reclining
stockings sagging   same bobbed hair as your nan

you tear out the guts of those VHS tapes
from your teens
and hang them from a streetlamp,
hoping this makeshift Maypole of black ribbon
distracts the mob approaching

now you're Gooseberry Bob
never raised a fist   like he did
but there are girls
locked in your screen

ale to dilute tears
sinking pints and pool balls
one day you'll be manly enough
to wear overalls…

here they come
rolling pins beating baking trays
animal clamour
the letterbox rattling
a bad case of nerves

* In the North of England, a procession would gather at dusk armed with
"culinary weapons", banging pots and pans, playing tin whistles, making
a general racket, carrying a youth on a length of wood (stang). This was
to recognise a "matrimonial difference" and make an example of a man
who beat his wife. The procession ended at the door of the unhappy
household where the youth would recite a song or poem (extracts taken
from *Punishments in the Olden Time* by William Andrews).

Jasmine Dreame Wagner

A Parliament of Leisures

I dream myself as other people.
They watch me,

and I watch me, and we
watch the sun

as the jets seed us.

They are not my fabrication, are not
images, nor are they words,

glass vials of futures.

The blight in the rearview mirror
is not a life I stumbled on.

And if I am to promise myself
an army, splendor,

a path for words to declassify.

If I am to steel blind magic.

+

In corridors,
the loneliness the cities touch

with heavy tools, with ink jet printers
whose processes glisten

like abs of mud
at low tide under piers.

Where fog rises, the world loses
its proprietary clasp on distances.

Children rehearse a flower's death.
Because they are awake, I am

a stray locked in a dream.

Which may be sung,
which must be sung,

or the world will shelter me.

+

Alone with a stranger,
an algorithm echoes

manufactured busyness.

A first-page political personality,
an evangelical network

trill over rounds of rage.

Where I speed,
their song's blades

flood the rural penmanship.

All my love to you
who are both law

and absent.

We, too
grow bold and break.

+

And in the event

the noise slips
from the fact of roads.

And in the event its absurd blood

is furious in the leaves.
And in the event the labor by which

the mind swings, repeating

a popular tune, stops
with the stillness of a traveler,

suddenly motionless.

In meter allotments of minutes.
Projects burn.

In music's adolescence.

Sleepless truths
shift.

+

It's true, I think I'm Eve.
I want only to follow

my instincts, drive the wax and feathers

from the embarrassed silence
on the other side of light.

Instinct first, then light. Then styrofoam

peanuts, inflatable mountains,
blow-up coasts. I think of

my seat belt

as though it is an extension
of myself. I'm nearly fiction

in the seams of this violent institution

in the detail in the fabrication
in the hushed cores of roads.

+

This is heroic, or so it seems.

And it seems for a long time.
And it seems for a very long time.

The detail in the fabrication

of the seams of institutions.
This where our hearts hide.

Where events' currents score us.

In the curvature of the earth.
In the hushed cores of heroes

there are no verified names.

Katherine Collins

Author's Note

A poem found in Annie Dillard's Mornings Like This.

I did not write a word of it. Other hands composed
the lines. Pawing through, they [held] and wave[ed]

aloft the element of broken text. I lifted them. Sometimes
I dropped the books themselves; and added original

intentions to a loose collection of torn and damaged
fragments. The baffling quality of spiritual knowledge

looks sober on the page. Consequently, I took
wild liberties, poetry's oldest and most sincere aim.

The Garden Is Bare, Except

for a Blenheim Orange rooted in tumbled gravel, fawn
except as the light strikes

the planes and minerals – silicates, carbonates, nitrates, borates –
all the colours crush onto a palette with the estrangement of
                                                    an abstract.
The tree is still,
except full of insubstantial movement fused intimately

in soundless struggle,
except the silence condenses into a glossary of precious

eyes and feathers, an enigmatic language of fluttering like scratches
on a window, opaque

except it reflects like blackwater and you can't tell if what you see
is the finest rain, dust, a cloud of midges in a faded evening.

I scrunch my eyes like tissue to extricate bird from leaf and branch,
except, as soon as I settle on one soft brown

shape it freezes – how do you recognise, thrush,
that flawless instant?

How Should One Live, to Please One's Biographer?

In a labyrinth of curled papers with the all the glory of a mediaeval city, your journals, humdrum bundles of incremental recollections, knotted up in crack-spined notebooks, lie

the dust, motes piling up like drifts undisturbed until a breath perturbs

in your biographers' attention. They contain your middle-moments, rinsed out in memory, lost or hurriedly

decaying, washed up in archives with cool passages that lead to anterooms where

your biographers convene amid the hard-backed chairs and peer at microfiches, fishing for slivers

of now. They blunder upon a time you gave all your attention to grief in a sudden flight like gulls in screeching trepidations and all comparable instances of joy are self-effacingly forgotten.

Mary Leader

Legacy

Has anyone seen Willeatha's madonna?
Her hands, her face, her feet, all of gold,
her gown, her veil, swirled all around
with baroque time, and her babe, also
of gold, draped with cloth from her hands
all hard and immobile ceramic, all experience
set. She has never been told who owns her
but knows she has been removed from her origin
where once, all on her shelf had
in common with her that parts of their bodies
or their haloes or the trim on their robes or the roses
that wreathed their feet were gold. No one
ever shifted, not even their gently-lowered gazes
but they sensed the comforting
presence of their neighbors. Who carried her
from her home, though? I know I
did not. Did she end up afraid in the dark
with strangers, somehow connected with sacrifice,
pushed to the back of a cabinet in Willeatha's
niece's niece's kitchen or isolated on a stand
in my mother's study or smothered accidentally,
in with my linens, or uncovered in a dream of
a grandmother's house, a multi-storied house
whose attic window afforded her
a view of angels working with gemstones?

Cards

1. How Catholics, who do believe in it, play cards

Ace, Deuce, Trey. Jack, Queen, King.
Granny Haddox, Great-Aunt Sara, and I.
Our three-handed game of Hearts every Sunday,

after Lunch, after Mass. Pastel dinner-mints,
and cashew-nuts, tea in the best bone china
cups&saucers, beautiful scrolls and flowers

tending to pink, rose, aqua, gold. Object: *avoid*
Hearts, a point each (lowest score wins, see).
Most important, avoid The Queen of Spades,

formidably known as "The Black Lady" –
She'll cost you 13 points! Unless
you can "Shoot the Moon," get *all* the hearts

and the queen of spades – that's 26 points
against each other player! Now in a four-handed
game, all 52 cards would be dealt, 13 each.

But in three-handed – 17 each, a total of 51 –
the spare card went "In the Kitty." Whoever
took the first Heart trick got the Kitty. Try

to imagine how nerve-wracking that was.
What if you were trying to shoot the moon
and the black lady was in the kitty?!

"Bless us and save us! said Mrs. O'Davis"

2. How Methodists, who don't believe in it, play cards

Simple numbers. 1 through 13. Instead of suits:
green, red, orange, black. Regular cards, as
amply evidenced by the terminology in section 1,
were Royalists! French! Papists! but what wickedness

could there be in integers and colors? Instead of
two jokers, two common crows, called "rooks" –
the game itself called "Rook." Beautiful unadorned
design, the rooks in stark black silhouette, like

Lincoln and Washington in February's classroom.
Grandma Privett and me, out in the country. Phone
the kind you crank. Now that I look at an actual deck –
they still make it – The Game of Rook, by Parker

Brothers, Salem, Massachusetts – I see the numbers
were 1-14, not 13, and there was one Rook, not two;
one Rook = two Jokers? the way one Queen of Spades
= thirteen Hearts? Whoa, in real life the colors were

green, red, black, and yellow. Yellow. Not orange,
as I had "remembered." Maybe I was conflating
the suits – I mean colors – with the sugar cookies
Grandma made, decorated with cut-up gumdrops:

green, red, orange. It could be she didn't use
the yellow ones because they wouldn't show up
very well against the pale dough, and nor, but for
the opposite reason, the black ones, lest they bleed

in the oven. Those, licorice-flavored, she saved –
this I hadn't recalled at all until now – for
my father, who'd have been in the sun room with
Bapaw. Licorice was Daddy's favorite, like me.

David Rushmer

Kindling

             transparency of
     the form

      that carries a body
I cannot separate from

    liquid night
    of graveyards

      hovering

      this sky

        & the music I chose
        from the inside and out

     interpreted and
        translated
        bliss

        your hand
        sounding
            the sunlight we are making

     "rubbing till your work is gone"

II

to disappear
    into
    forms

        between
        speech
        roots

        and
silences
    to come
        spark across bridges
          collapsing

to catch one's breath
        in a mirror
           of rain

conceiving
    the mind
    in each
    droplet

    into likeness
        of likeness

        collision, *of fragments*

          "to burn up, in a gesture
          outside the body"

from White Drift

I

      air

aflame in the wind

          open mouthed

.

blood sews the voice
          with white needle

.

          your shadow
               recognizes you
     in the passage through
     veins blossomed

.

my mouth skins

      buried light

II

.

      darkness thorned

             between the face
      &
      your scream
      below
             the fingers

.

             the sky
                    hangs

      under your breath

.

blackbirds
      drifting night

mouthed
      the sorrow blown
      substance

Carrie Etter

Youth

On the city's edge   on the other side   of a wall of trees
a cathedral city   in the tall grasses   we grasped grappled gasped
kissed and licked   a pale winter sun   arms and legs and lips and
eyes   sighed and struck and fumbled   O joyous   impatience

Forty-Some Days

There never was a daughter.
The farm cats grew feral after –
Six weeks before the flood waters subsided –

Boy, boy, boy, boy.
She'd reached to pet the mother, her special one, and –
Six weeks of water, six months of –

She let their hair grow long, longer than he –
Each time, such thin lines of red.
The mind-blotting work of it.

She strove to hold them close, but not too –
She put out more food, more bedding, apology upon apology.
"God?" she murmured without recognition.

No one asked after the crop, the harvest.
At the post office, at the grocer,
she swapped nods without blinking.

Mark Dickinson

Friend Request

A bald man dreams of hair and wakes up disappointed, clouds are no substitute and the wilderness, if it can be called that, is problematic. When I dress like a thrush I constantly quiver. With each new corruption the monotony of self pervades the snowcapped blossom. The words, "I love you" are vivid in autumn, but I'm not prepared to have a discussion on the subject at this time. I opened the curtains so the sun could shine on the righteous. In my garden (note the possessive) I saw a blackcap. Snow buntings gather in the field and I intrude on their moment, they take flight, settle and watch me from a safer distance. Vegans should pay attention to sources of organic phosphorus; origins can be problematic. Corrosive Economics are pervading the tundra in search of delirium. As a child I was beaten so badly my skin turned red, blue, black, green, yellow. In the present the trauma of force seeps into microscopic rainbows which become vivid and deep in winter. Behind the force of a coal shovel lay intent. Happiness is complicated and requires a sheltered spot with protection against hard borders. Everything seems perpetually messy. But the plough has shaped the soil so the structure is new. If you tilt your head ever so slightly to the left, you'll see complexity through simplicity. I am over whelmed by facts and figures but underwhelmed when trying to participate. Only scripted narratives make sense. I hover over the water in a pattern of light & dark. Show me your clichés and I'll buy you a drink [slow breathing, muffled sounds – yet audible]. The path is overgrown with mixed forage grasses and Wordsworth's mutable finitude, it leads to a theory of abandonment, which is incomplete, leaning toward a resolution of entanglement, stretched from the Holocene into this relational depth. As light rips gently into the future it does so with impressive fluidity. Small stones dark with rain. I trespass at your window & reimagine your past, my intrusion becomes a fantasy of apparitions drowning in a water feature. Nothing makes me happy but, "I love you".

Unsubscribe

Tears ambush the central reservation and I'm not sure what to do about it. Living ethically is proving to be expensive, but with enough money 'self-sufficiency' becomes an option. Subscribing to the law of attraction I focused on a wind turbine and the universe brought me a large colourful holographic windmill to stick in the sand. I don't like cutting myself, but occasionally I will punch myself repeatedly in the face. Honesty is the best policy, unless it's the worst. Now I have your attention I want to mention urban acidification and tree adaptability. I am dreaming of scrub savannah at the tree-limit, where islands of crooked wood stretch the horizontal through apical termination, as resource gains exceed the losses by the thinnest of margins. There are many lessons to surviving at the extremes of tolerance. Thin calls with a touch of orange flutter momentarily. I have thoughts on violence as the intellectualised or creative use of excess. I grow many types of flower but primrose (vulgaris) is native, yet should not be considered an indicator of ancient woodland. I find the appearance of dwarf willow in the verges curious. I'm inclined to snatch small animals from the surface of water, but focus instead on the sunshine yellow of the daffodil and the cold north wind that desiccates. When I was little he hit you, I blamed myself but the lupins which aren't native bring fresh optimism to the colour blue. Lupins in Iceland are becoming invasive, but today I want to focus on a positive and the efficiency of interaction between different nodule bacteria in relation to the variability of nitrogen fixation. But realistically I'm more likely to follow an alarm call against humans that's a dry rasping scream among intermittent hints of blue & yellow.

Rioting in Comfort

I dressed in a party frock rioting through the small affections of conformity with melancholic pre-assembled speech bubbles that made me feel awkward. In the living room a new theatre of wilderness paraded its evergreens through pre-existing harmonies of colour. At the limit of love trailing through binary stars I brushed against anthers strained by distance like a falsetto bark.

Delete-Delete

Now that the musics on standby and nobodies home I want to rub
myself in a new kind of sadness. Where anxiety accompanies the
fresh bright empty through paradisical incompleteness to a place
that's simply not robust enough to pirouette through the crisis, or
shimmy through its glittering deletions. At each emptying injunctive,
the sweet vowel meadows and consonants of wilderness dally in
disappearance and spread to inelegant blank space. Bleating this
strangeness, the surface of my eyes will mirror scraps of yesterday
painting the coastal frescoes with denatured love which impacts the
climate. Down wind my wings at a distance amplify the hum knitted
in a lullaby of mutations and threats. With tongue on fire disturbance
beams the pith of contusion and little fears which stalk the landscapes
monotonous tracts, stain the harmonies with glimmering distress and
consume to a fraction.

Out of tune

*Leaning against a tiny discreet petal, our window on the obvious sounds
like a mistimed overture accompanied by the prising of metal. In ministered
convulsions modified in the revelations of mist gathered on the summit of
climate, we drift through portals of glitter, into gutters of transport discharging
to disappointment. Our Inserts of fetish found then lost, link back to a status
which continued to reinvent itself post-death. How in this sphere of porous
calamities, did graceful inserts subject to submissive tropes, become gilt fondled
hems denatured & forever reinvented? Nothing of this music screens behind
the glass of unwelcome, now that the sill of margins is selective mute and the
cost of belonging, embossed in digits, balances the snow white purity on the
unseasonal sheet.*

Isobel Armstrong

Four Rilke Elegies

Orpheus   beyond   sings   into being
the rose-bowl's silver calyx   conjures
                    O *deictic spectral rose's not thereness*
the opening eyelids of each rose
whorl-layer swirl-layer flushed
gentle geometry   delicate capillaries vein petal tissue
                    pure voids of the calculus   pure   voids   O
self-enclosing helix furled round a   cavity
                    rose made of emptiness
petal's cadence   *made from spaces   rhythm depends on*   sing
the dead's invidia paused awhile
the harsh intransigent angel forgiving   the   the   the
a space

1914-18
'how this disaster has squandered us'
mud-blood-gorged
lavishes eviscerate torso   spendthrift dismembered limbs   dis
remembered stumps   Deutsche Heer   refuse
requiem's reparation   disremem   coronach   monody
'a revolt in their minds against mourning'   mourning our
            indemnity   our getout   dismem
war murder   murderers of ourselves   dis-mem   re   inducted
in hate's efficiency   spilled abdomen   mem   dis
remem   a paean to itself   hate   trained in raptures of loathing
primal severance   dis   congeals   hate's symbols
impossible   requiem's immunity for the million dead   dis-bered
re-re-re   mem-mem-mem-re   only a death-bell vibrating
            interstellar space
to the bone

82

why did he turn back?
the lyre lost its nerve   soft crepuscular shades treading
hades soft shades crepuscular   soft shades   treading soft crepuscular
crepuscular soft   hades   shades   soft
treading crepuscular   hades   soft shades
nerve lost   the lyre
turn back   back turn
treading shades crepuscular soft
crepuscular soft treading   shades soft crepuscular   shades soft hades
soft   shades   hades   soft   crepuscular
shades soft   hades   crepuscular treading
lyre   the lost nerve
why?

spray-spume   springs   re-making   forever
turning itself into sky
air understands water
re-traces a fountain's exhalation   marble's memories
breathing   winds and breezes recognise   re-remember
in green coverts   or   remorseless city stones' sun-glare
yet
there's water and alabaster entwined
breathing   you'd think
water matter   stone in flux   exchanging transparency and
          gravitas   veined
alabaster and water amour
marble immemorial murmur
of conch and shell

Gad Hollander

from Identity Diagrams and Other IDs

Impersonation Document

He had one hundred ID's, more or less, his pockets replete with divers Identity Diagrams. One hundred – less than stars in the sky but more than a handful of pebbles – the default conceptual number, suggesting that his more-than-a-few-but-not-so-many identities each retained its anonymity, and the chances of any one ID encountering another on any given day were virtually zero. Yet even if such an unlikely conjunction had ever occurred, it would have been noted, duly recorded under the rubric *Imaginary Digressions*, rendered a pure fantasy. Which is why, to avoid falling into a parallel universe ordered by a parallel logic, as well as for obvious security reasons, we ask every passer-by, regardless of assumed Identity: who, actually, deep down, are you?

Invisible Disguises

Café. A man & a woman with a new-born baby seated at a table; another man with a baby sits down at the next table. The woman talks to the man – relentlessly, excitedly, at speed – about her child & all kinds of baby accessories. The man responds enthusiastically with his own thoughts on the subject. Their dialogue morphs into a duet, a recitative listing baby items: she citing from her favourite catalogues while he proffers alternatives from other sources: an elastic bouncer, a buggy, an electric pacifier. They focus exclusively, ineluctably, on infanthood; we have no idea what else might occupy their lives or if there's any subtext to their chatting. Meanwhile, the woman's partner has slipped away quietly, ordering coffee at the counter. Why such fanatical devotion to nappies & dummies here, in a café, within earshot of a miserable old scribbler mired in complex sentences, forever on the lookout for his *mot juste*? It's all so tedious, so self-absorbed, this dotage on inarticulate, if sentient, beings – as it would be! And although we can forgive them this obsessive yet natural interest in their offspring, we take exception to their seemingly insatiable need to debate every facet of their newfound parenthood in public; we would prefer them to simply be and interact with their respective sprogs, both sound asleep in their prams as we scribble. [In "The Sun Placed in The Abyss", Francis Ponge describes his "we" as a succession of I's in different places & positions – to which we would add: mental states.] What's more, the woman's high-pitched staccato barrage, her grating verbal attrition, tests the acoustic limits of the café and leaves us, leaves me, praying for either infant to wake up & cry out: for food, for comfort, for some human warmth. But neither of them does; they remain peacefully submerged under the droning blather of their progenitors' comingling voices, their subconscious worlds swathed in a flood of verbiage seeping though their soft, impressionable skulls as their home environments are subtly reshaped and new realities appear, as if through the gurgling spittle of their short breaths – "is *he* my new papa? *she* my new mama?" – although a blissful ignorance and perfect innocence pervade the café air thanks, of course, to our scribbler's unimpeachable say-so.

Idlyllic Depictions (The Pondification of Water)

"Through memory we travel against time, through forgetfulness we follow its course." Joseph Joubert (1789)

a blanket of algae covered the pond this morning –
whereas yesterday it was bare & reflective

> three kingfishers
> by the pond –
> spotted only
> one: a
> flash of ochre/blue
> in the foliage
> in the distance

Wrecked love has left a rusted old car at the bottom of a drained pond, half-buried in 40-year-old mud, awaiting the authorities, or the gods, to deal with it, whoever comes first.

Light morning rain: a heron glides along the length of the pond, wings outstretched, coming to rest on the far bank; perched among low bending branches, it closes its wings, stays dead still, head & neck immobile, eyes open, beak shut, shrouded in soft mist or light rain.

The pond intermittently sprayed by fine rain; the morning creating an elemental but fleeting union of things.

Idyllic day this morning at the pond – the heron stood perfectly straight, like a signpost, among the rushes on the far side. Unless I imagined it.

A pair of herons flew over the pond this morning, one just skimming the water, the other a few meters above it. They traversed the entire length of the far bank, then veered off in opposite directions, one to the right, the other to the left, both sweeping upward, following the lay of the land – perhaps returning to their respective nests from a clandestine tryst in the tall reeds. Moments later a seagull began to attack the coot's nest in the middle of the pond, inside one of the rings, but was beaten off by the mother. The gull swerved away, circled overhead, then landed & perched itself atop one of the concrete pillars at the end of the pier, looking stupidly (or pensively) at the water as it tried to work out its next move.

Asked this morning what I do, I said: I'm a writer and procrastinator. That is, I write, then pause to think between every other word. Like thinking, but without the uninterrupted flow.

Víctor Manuel Mendiola

translated by Timothy Adès

The hard-boiled egg

I take the frail egg from the woven wicker.
Its weight is on my hand, its base is round,
it's white and weightless, taciturn, profound,
it's medieval, it is gold and ogre.

It's in the spoon – the pan is on the cooker;
I plunge it in the fury and the sound,
the timer's on; timidity is drowned;
it's old and hard with new and febrile vigour.

The whole thing has the pure white form of terror.
The puncturing's trapped in the never-never,
the cockerel is humbled in the slammer:

the egg's not in his song, it's in some other.
The gold is tough enough without the ogre;
the egg, grown old and hardened, is my supper.

El huevo duro

De la cestilla tomo el frágil huevo.
Sobre la mano pesa su redondo
blanco sin peso – tan callado y hondo,
tan oro y ogro como un medioevo.

Con la cuchara hasta el perol lo llevo
y el tiempo mido; en el hervor lo escondo
y miro cómo el miedo baja al fondo;
ser viejo y duro es un febril renuevo.

Todo es la blanca forma del espanto.
Atrapada la nunca picadura
y el gallo a la mazmorra reducido,

es el huevo la nota de otro canto
y oro sin ogro guarda la armadura;
mi cena, el duro huevo envejecido.

Ivano Fermini

translated by Ian Seed

from Banished White

I say and we mix our hands
I take from a cloud
but then the ash fills
war's tombstones
here is the one I loved on a line
move a streak of lightning
so that a doll you bounce off the columns
poetry leans out I tell you
if dust and the like are in a mantle
my paper as a brake
I will tell the sky then… I have a swollen eye
the old people unwrap and whistle at the honey
the water which dries laughing

★

high covers as if closing spring in a sphere of smoke
would-be cabriolets the thought punched through the wet masks
……in a….
…the cuts of places….
…grey design: wood: the most essential escape
poets it is as I say
some flour's left askew then it's a small girl who touches your hair
until its falling reaches into the dark
the spiders are hurled for mum   it's   Sunday

★

the jokes which appear in seeds
which cut canals in paper and clothes
we will love several times

more is a rock to soften
the torch on the face of entire tastes
o doves! icily!
everything I no longer know how to remain with
and coriander calls for similar vapours
here is the kiss for you which leaps several times

which advances without saying anything
the elastic of the throne

★

in following the forest to his light teeth
who has thought in the bark has seen
as when I stick myself to the pile
and you go off to one side of the stamp without earth
so then it attaches itself to the slab the head
smashed by straw-coloured races
but you don't want to whistle on your own account

metal which goes to the south!

cherry which stays in the north!

I will give you a snowstorm and white

★

one white side with logs
dart past together
and pyjama and carrot crash against stone
I too have entered this circular violence
poet! now I have attained the stage of the man who walks slowly
and I push away the saving produced in the bitterness of a sling
but who knows how to return
that falls indifferently between the pieces of the flood
and I will love forever the death of snow

★

and away towards a climbing into the air
having let your hand slip into the flood
leaves therefore bear a title
boats of tools and lamps to love as they are
I know how to describe you infinitely in the garden
with the thief of peace who hangs around the profitable side
on this table the buzz of pebbles
the trumpets of murderous places

*

were men and vapours on a detour
through the rooms a false circle
nevertheless I ask for a fly to climb
the rot and rust
as the leaves which are in him
can lock themselves in and give bread to our ribs
what was that seed
weeps in silence and I chain myself to fire
and when will it be
a lily on my shoulder, my face with its sudden pain

Celia Parra

translated by Patrick Loughnane

Four Poems

You analyse
the cartography of their voice
in the processor.

You love
the peaks and valleys
that their accent makes
as one can only love
a bundle of pixels and decibels:
with the force of someone who clings
to the touch of the image,
that which can't be handled.

That dense plateau is their laugh
saturating the signal.
That valley,
a silence
in which perhaps a gaze lowers
and a hand is passing through hair.

The most beautiful curve,
the parabola of that vowel that gently drags
at the end of the word
at the end of the sentence
like a leaf that falls from a tree
and glides
until it kisses the ground.

★

It always starts with a tremor.
A constant whistling
at high frequencies.

Screens announce it obsessively
for days in advance
– electrical storm between four and five AM,
please remain indoors –.

Then comes the interference.

Everything the eyes see
dissolves into shifting edges
– what our ancestors called a glitch –.
Colour bursts into a frenzy
and it's hard to have a hold of the body.

During those hours
the toothed recesses of the clouds are
terribly dangerous,
a train could derail onto the bar terrace
and the house
arch itself several kilometres out to sea
and then
return intact.

★

By day
screens can't compete with the brightness of the LED
and are mirrors.

To see yourself like this
veiled with images
as though a body was only that which delimits
the edge of a screen.
A shadow continuum.
A river.

You lift your feet to look at yourself
and fall
into the reflection.

The mirror shows a world
that fits into your hand.

Hard to tell what's real.

★

When you smile,
from the edge of your eyes emerge
timid streams of shadow.
On-screen,
Every wrinkle is the crack
that split Pangaea.

So you learned from the dam to stifle expressions.
To keep yourself intact before the tyranny of the pixel.

You know that here nothing escapes
high resolution,
high
definition:
Panopticon.

Vaiva Grainytė

translated by Rimas Uzgiris

Autumn, 2009

Autumn's ripped belly pushes gifts on us:
not sales on coats (as we wished), but zucchinis.

Autumn's swollen breasts barge into our mouths:
we suckle on rain, not milk.

Autumn's finger commands we clean the environment:
we rake up murdered judges instead of leaves.

Occupiers – colds and polyps – share our nasal septums:
the left is for *her*, the right is for *him* (is the nose the case of
Vilnius is ours and we are Russia's?)

Only the owl is copacetic in this season:
it fluffs its pretty down feathers up.

Wind So Strong

The wind so strong:
jellyfish have gathered into a single jellybush,
drying clothes have broken the laundry string's spine,
mosquitos have been swept from ceiling perches,
and my head has been blown onto your bed.

Not the Fire Shift

The chicks, now being fed on corals,
ran into the boulevard and began to eat everything:
trees
weeds
and dead-end streets
shop-windows
sidewalks
newsstands
and kiosks
casinos
bistros
houses
cafés
and cafeterias
courtyards
bars
barber shops
restaurants
laundromats
tobacconists
coffee clubs
tea houses
libraries
music stores
video stores
movie theatres
and theatre theatres.

So why have you gone nuts, my speckled ones, I ask.
Not nuts, not nuts at all, for today we're starting a fire.

To Each His Own

I know what will happen
when we meet:
we will circle on the Pope's former track
(in Confluence Park, by the exercise bars
where during gym class we had to stretch
our little joints, and the Pope held Mass).
You will tell me again
how nothing is working out:
employers don't pay on time,
clients don't like the layouts,
you got in a fight again with A.,
A. has moved out.
The dog whimpers annoyingly
in the mornings, and has gotten too big
for the kitchen.

Then it will be my turn to speak:
I'll list the countries recently visited,
grants newly granted.
I'll dictate the facts which dictate my success
and how much of the world I see
(leaving out my journeys through clinic corridors
and the offices of dark thoughts).

And the monkey from the Mulhouse Zoo
will continue to eat his creamed kiwis,
pooping away the elevenses of captivity:
to each his own.

Kęstutis Navakas

translated by Rimas Uzgiris

*

in the shoes wherein there are no toes
footprints do not register. the sleeves lack
arms. hair soaks up all thought which can then
be found in the teeth of combs. the mirror will
always fall face first. shafts of light don't reflect
from it's prone shield of darkness. the king is dead
with powder in his wrinkles. the word forest
does not contain a single letter. a drunk glass of wine
loses all meaning while drunk wine takes it all in.
what trickles from my fingernails are the shavings
of the points of iron nails. the skeletons inside of you
my dear have been sleeping for twenty years

together with mine. twenty years which also are not:
it's just a number lacking all wrinkles and powder

★

plants are portuguese. animals are
french. metals are german and
minerals scandinavian. natural phenomena
from central europe probably once
belonged to the habsburgs. what we
do is jewish. what we think
depends. if good then czech if bad then
albanian or italian. if nothing then swiss
or belgian. our passions are spanish
our silence is icelandic our faith
is polish our subconscious is ancient greek.
our love – all the vanished nations.

no brits. no hungarians. no russians or dutch.
no lithuanians. they were left unwritten

★

why those axes. the meaning of axes is too
obscure. why saws and damask steel
it's not always possible to comprehend scissors either
but they're beautiful. it's not always possible to
enter a room when scissors lie on the table.
there are not always rooms that you can just
enter. but everything can be cut through or
chopped with a paper's edge if it contains
at least two letters. one is not enough.
one alone has nothing to lean on and will fall
through it's own abyss. if you manage
to find a second – don't wait. let it in:

you'll chop with the paper's edge. then axes will be
lowered and blood will have time to coagulate

★

today chimed twelve at half past three
today you saw people who aren't witnessed
by clocks. they were free people
like those in bosch's hell and they no longer
possessed fear of being mugged by time
so they danced in a circle sometimes
holding hands you couldn't make out
any features to their faces except …
sometimes the water flared and
kept rising until the sea reached the brown
scratch on the … which was then burned by the sun
and the waves crackled while fish swam in schools

wanting to melt as the bell rang and people
happily let paper boats go down with the ship

★

sleep. i've pecked out your eyes even though
they had no nutritional value. sleep. the shutters
are already shut and coffee has become

grounds the trees today are empty only
a lonely maple runs down the street we
don't follow him with our eyes we

are enough for us. we are real. everything
else is stolen according to osc w. and there is no
everything else. there never was. even now i

don't know why you don't sicken me. slee

Notes on Contributors

TIMOTHY ADÈS is well-known for his metrical, rhyming translations from French and Spanish. Shearsman published his edition of the selected poetry of Alfonso Reyes, *Miracle of Mexico*, in 2019.

MARTIN ANDERSON appeared in the very first issue of *Shearsman* magazine in 1981, and is still here. His most recent publications are *Ice Stylus* (2017) and the chapbook, *In the Empire of Chimeras* (2018), both from Shearsman.

ISOBEL ARMSTRONG is a renowned scholar and critic of 19th-century poetry, literary theory and woman's writing, and is an emeritus professor at Birkbeck University in London. Her most recent books are, *Victorian Glassworlds. Glass Culture and the Imagination* (2008), which won the Modern Language Association's James Russell Lowell Prize in 2009, and *Novel Politics: Democratic Imaginations in Nineteenth-Century Fiction* (2016). A second edition of her seminal study *Victorian Poetry: Poetry, Poetics and Politics* appeared in 2019.

SARAH BARNSLEY's publications include the pamphlet, *The Fire Station* (Telltale Press, 2015), and a selection of literary criticism. A senior lecturer at Goldsmiths, University of London, Sarah lives in Hove.

JAMES BELL is Scottish and now lives in France where he contributes photography and non-fiction to an English language journal. His third poetry collection *Here At The End Of The World* is forthcoming from Lapwing. He has been contributing poetry to *Shearsman* magazine since the mid-noughties.

KATHERINE COLLINS is a poet from Bristol. She works at the University of Oxford, where she holds a Leverhulme Fellowship; her writing has appeared in *Finished Creatures, Ink Sweat & Tears*, and *Anthropocene*.

JENNIFER K. DICK is an author with three books, most recently *Lilith: A Novel in Fragments* (Corrupt, 2019) and a fourth appearing in London this year: *That Which I Touch Has No Name*. She writes an irregular column called *Of Tradition and Experiment* for *Tears in the Fence*, and teaches American Lit and Civ at the Université de Haute Alsace in Mulhouse, France.

MARK DICKINSON's *Tender Geometries* was published by Shearsman in 2015. He lives in the Orkneys.

CARRIE ETTER recently published *The Weather in Normal,* her fourth full-length collection (Seren, in the UK; Station Hill Press, in the USA, 2019).

IVANO FERMINI (1948-2004) spent most of his life in Milan. He is the author of two collections, both long out of print. *the straw which comes apart,* a translation of a short selection of Fermini's poems, was published in a bilingual edition by Oystercatcher Press (2010).

AMLANJYOTI GOSWAMI's poetry has been published around the world, in India, Nepal, Bangladesh, Hong Kong, the UK, USA, South Africa, Kenya and Germany, and in the anthologies, *40 under 40: An Anthology of Post Globalisation Poetry* (Poetrywala), *A Change of Climate* (Manchester Metropolitan University, Environmental Justice Foundation and the University of Edinburgh) and the *Sahitya Akademi Anthology of Modern English Poetry*. His recent collection of poems, *River Wedding*, was published by Poetrywala in 2019 and has been widely reviewed. His poems have also appeared on street walls of Christchurch, exhibitions in Johannesburg and buses in Philadelphia. He has read in various places, including in New York, Delhi and Boston. He grew up in Guwahati, Assam, and lives in Delhi.

VAIVA GRAINYTĖ is a Lithuanian poet, librettist and dramatist, working for both stage and radio. Her most recent collection is *Gorilla Archives* (*Gorilos archyvai*, Vilnius: Lithuanian Writers' Union Publishing House, 2019).

RALPH HAWKINS has a long list of publications to his name, including three volumes from Shearsman, the latest of which is *It Looks Like an Island But Sails Away* (2015).

CHRIS HOLDAWAY was once a pupil of Shearsman author Lisa Samuels at Auckland University. His work is mostly found in the US, where he obtained his MFA at Notre Dame. Now back in New Zealand, he directs the chapbook publisher, Compound Press.

GAD HOLLANDER is an American writer and film-maker living in London. His books include *Benching with Virgil* (Avec Books, 2000) and *The Palaver* (with Andrew Bick, Book Works, 1998).

ANDREW JORDAN has two collections from Shearsman, the most recent of which is *Hegemonick* (2012).

LISA KELLY's first collection, *A Map Towards Fluency*, was published by Carcanet in June 2019. Her pamphlets are *Philip Levine's Good Ear* (Stonewood Press) and *Bloodhound* (Hearing Eye).

MARY LEADER recently retired from university teaching, and lives in Oklahoma. Her most recent Shearsman collection is *She Lives There Still* (2018).

Rosanna Licari is an Australian poet and writer. Her work has appeared in various Australian and international publications, including previous issues of this magazine. In 2019, she completed a Residential Fellowship at Varuna, The National Writers' House, and is the poetry editor of online literary journal, *StylusLit*. UQP published her book, *An Absence of Saints*, in 2010.

PATRICK LOUGHNANE is a poet and translator. He has translated Galician poets for festivals across Europe. His translation work was most recently featured in the anthology *Wretched Strangers* (Boiler House Press, 2018).

VÍCTOR MANUEL MENDIOLA's *Selected Poems* was published by Shearsman under the title *Your hand, my mouth* in 2008. The poem here was also published in that volume in an unrhymed translation by Ruth Fainlight

ABEGAIL MORLEY's fourth collection, *The Skin Diary* is published by Nine Arches Press (2016). Her debut collection, *How to Pour Madness into a Teacup* (2010) was shortlisted for the Forward Prize Best First Collection. *The Unmapped Woman* is forthcoming from Nine Arches Press. She is co-editor of Against the Grain Press and editor of *The Poetry Shed*.

KĘSTUTIS NAVAKAS won all the major poetry awards in Lithuania, as well as the National Prize for Culture and the Arts. He is a poetic landmark there, rarely published in English, though his *Šimtas du* [One Hundred Two], from which the poems here are taken, has been translated recently into German. He passed away in February 2020, just after these translations were accepted for publication.

CELIA PARRA is a Galician poet, born in Ourense in 1990, and the poems here are all drawn from her second collection, *Pantallas* (Galaxia, 2018). Her work has been much anthologised and she has read at festivals in Germany and Ireland as well as in her native Spain.

SIMON PERCHIK (b. 1923), like Martin Anderson, has been appearing in *Shearsman* since the magazine first began. He lives on Long Island, NY, and his many books include a collected edition, *Hands Collected* (Pavement Saw Press, Columbus, OH, 2000) and *The Osiris Poems* (box of chalk, 2017). Cholla Needles (Joshua Tree, CA) have published two further books since the latter appeared.

MEGHAN PURVIS received an MA and PhD from the University of East Anglia, and an MFA from North Carolina State University. Her translation of *Beowulf* was published in 2013 and won the 2011 *Times* Stephen Spender Prize for literary translation. She is currently working on her first novel.

PETER ROBINSON's *Collected Poems* was published by Shearsman in 2017. A volume of essays on his work is also in development here, edited by Tom Philips.

DAVID RUSHMER's first full-length collection, *Remains to Be Seen*, was published by Shearsman in 2018.

IAN SEED's latest collection of poetry is *New York Hotel* (Shearsman, 2018). His translations include *The Thief of Talant*, from the French of Pierre Reverdy (Wakefield, 2016), and *Bitter Grass*, from the Italian of Gëzim Hajdari (Shearsman, 2020). Shearsman will publish his new collection, *The Underground Cabaret*, in late 2020.

NATHAN SHEPHERDSON is the author of five books of poetry. He has collaborated with artists and writers including Pascalle Burton, Alun Leach-

Jones and Sandra Selig. His current project is with Berlin-based artist Arryn Snowball, utilising the reference book *Grant's Guide to Fishes*.

HAZEL SMITH is a British-Australian poet, performer and new media artist who lives in Sydney. From 2007-2017 Hazel was a Research Professor at Western Sydney University, where she is now an Emeritus Professor. She has published four volumes of poetry, including *Word Migrants* (Giramondo, Sydney, 2016) and *The Erotics of Geography* (Tinfish, Honolulu, 2008).

JENNIFER SPECTOR is a poet born and raised in New York City, living in Panama since 1998. Her work explores the poetics of language in relation to landscape and the natural world. Her poetry has been also been included in chapbooks, such as *Nature & Sentience* (Corbel Stone Press), *Book of Hours:An Artist's Book for the Anthropocene* (Artist Rebecca Clark), and *Suelo* (Estudio Nuboso). Her website is at: www.jenniferspectorstudio.com

MATTHEW HEDLEY STOPPARD is the UK's first official Town Poet in Otley, West Yorkshire. He has two collections published by Valley Press, the first, *A Family Behind Glass*, was a *Guardian* Readers' Book of the Year.

RIMAS UZGIRIS is a poet, translator, editor and critic. He is a busy translator of Lithuanian poetry, including *Vagabond Sun,* an edition of Judita Vaičiūnaitė, for Shearsman (2018). He teaches translation at Vilnius University, and recently published his own first collection, *North of Paradise* (Kelsay Books).

JASMINE DREAME WAGNER is the author of *On a Clear Day* (Ahsahta Press), a collection of lyric essays and poems.

G.C. WALDREP teaches at Bucknell University in Pennsylvania and edits the journal *West Branch*. His most recent books are *feast gently* (Tupelo Press, 2018) and the long poem *Testament* (BOA Editions, 2015).